W9-AUY-696

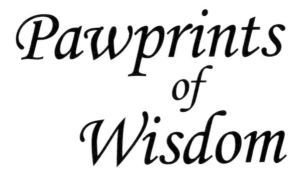

Pawprints
of
Wisdom

Copyright © 2015 by Carol Grace Anderson.

All rights reserved. No part of this publication may be reproduced, stored in a retrieval system or transmitted in any form or by any means, electronic, mechanical, photocopying, recording or otherwise, without the written permission of the publisher.

ISBN: 978-1-59842-903-9

◾ and Blue Mountain Press are registered in U.S. Patent and Trademark Office. Certain trademarks are used under license.

Printed in China.
Third Printing: 2016

♻ This book is printed on recycled paper.

This book is printed on paper that has been specially produced to be acid free (neutral pH) and contains no groundwood or unbleached pulp. It conforms with the requirements of the American National Standards Institute, Inc., so as to ensure that this book will last and be enjoyed by future generations.

Blue Mountain Arts, Inc.
P.O. Box 4549, Boulder, Colorado 80306

Pawprints
of
Wisdom

Life Lessons
from Our Dogs

Carol Grace Anderson, MA

Blue Mountain Press™
Boulder, Colorado

Introduction

Sometimes we don't find our new dog—she finds us. That's how I met my first fur baby, Cowgirl. After she had made several visits to my front door for a treat and a bowl of water, I got attached to this beautiful, muddy, matted stray. We searched for her family, but soon realized that now WE were family.

Cowgirl was not only a special gift—she also taught me some lessons about life that I'll treasure forever. I'm sure you can relate to what your angel with four paws has taught you. This little book is a reminder.

— Carol Grace Anderson

Lesson One: Flexibility

Dogs are amazingly flexible.
Do you notice how they adjust to our schedules?
Our lifestyles? Our changing circumstances?
They don't whine—they just go with the flow.

Change is inevitable, and it's constant, too, so we might as well get used to it. We may not embrace change, because it's uncomfortable, but we can be resilient creatures, and life's demands ease up when we learn how to be more adaptable.

Having a dog helps us become more flexible. All of a sudden, unless we have a fenced-in yard, we may be faced with walking in the rain or snow to give him his outside break. We may have to make an unexpected visit to the veterinarian's office when we're short on time or find a pet-care solution when we go out of town.

When it's a priority, we become pretty good at finding alternatives. We really can't control all our circumstances and challenges, but we can control our decisions, actions, and reactions. That's very powerful when you think about it.

If we were only half as resilient as our dogs, our lives would be lots easier. Just think of how easy and natural it is for dogs to bounce right back after we've had to reprimand them. It's as though they're thinking, *Okay, that's over. Now we're great friends again. Let's play!*

Or how about when we walk our dog down a new, unfamiliar path? They're probably thinking, *Oh, we're going this way today—how cool.* You're busy and have work to do? They're thinking, *I'll take a nap and try for some attention a little later.* Of course they don't forget to try again—and soon.

Things happen all day long in our lives that are beyond our control. Let's be as flexible as our dogs are. It works so much better!

Lesson Two: Confidence

Fear will discourage our dreams
and detour our progress.

I suspect that your furry friend would happily take on a mixed pack of wolves, coyotes, and tigers if given the opportunity, truly believing in victory. That's confidence!

We humans have learned to live in fear. We're born with very few innate fears—such as the fear of falling and the fear of loud noise. Most other fears are learned, starting at a very young age.

The good news is that, of course, we can unlearn our fears and live more confidently. We just have to do something different to get a different result. The only way is to begin to take more confident actions today. Starting a little at a time, new behaviors spark more new behaviors. It's a positive process.

Sure, we all need some fear to be safe. We don't want to jump in front of a train, fall out of a tree, or drive without seatbelts. But we do want to jump out of our comfort zone and take healthy risks to live more confidently.

By taking small, new steps consistently, we can overcome our fears just like we did when we learned to walk. Feel the fear and take those new steps. In time, they'll become safe and familiar. We just have to start. Now.

Our dogs approach every new person and experience with interest and curiosity. No fear. No judgment. When it comes to living fearlessly and confidently, our furry friends wrote the book.

Let's follow their lead.

Lesson Three: Laughter

Dogs find great joy in the simplest things.
They're thrilled it's morning!

They say laughter is the best medicine, and it's true. And isn't it interesting that, in time, we can find something funny about even the most difficult circumstances? Think of your funniest holiday or vacation experiences. They're about how wrong things went—am I right?

We don't always remember the smooth, expected, lovely moments, but we never forget the crazy, unpredictable experiences. They were usually the most fun!

One Saturday afternoon, I was walking with Cowgirl in a field near a church. There was a wedding going on, and the front door of the church was open. Cowgirl went over to check things out. Before I knew what was happening, she had walked right in and started following the bride! By the time I could get to her (I didn't want to yell), she was halfway down the aisle—tail wagging all the way. Apparently she thought everyone was gathered to celebrate her!

When we finally got outside, she looked up at me with a *what's-the-big-deal?* look. I was so embarrassed, but what was there to do but have a good, hearty laugh? In time, it would be a fun story for the wedding couple… I hoped.

When we're caught up in the stressed-out details of life, our pets remind us to chill out. Notice how they know the exact times to step in? They're funny without even trying to be—without saying one word!

If we can just allow ourselves to be more comfortable with being silly sometimes, we'll reap big benefits.

Lesson Four: Exercise

*The good news is that dogs need regular exercise...
and that means every single day.*

This need for daily exercise was a rude awakening
to my leisurely morning routine of coffee and the
newspaper in my bathrobe. Now I had to get up, get
dressed, and get out there a-walkin'.

More good news is that some beautiful stuff can
happen out in nature. For instance, I never realized
how enchanting a walk in light rain can be. It is
mysterious and energizing, and it provides a good
facial moisturizer to boot!

If it weren't for faithfully walking my dog, I
wouldn't have experienced the beauty of each
season, such as the fragrance of lilacs and sweet
honeysuckle bursting into spring blooms.

Summer mornings can be lively with clusters of kids
playing nearby, and chances are that your puppy
will be thrilled to visit with them.

Autumn is loaded with brilliant color, fresh scents in the air, and sometimes the blaring sounds of a high school band practicing for their halftime show.

Even the clear, cold morning air in winter is a powerful wake-up call to start the day. Our furry friends don't seem to mind it at all.

We know from health experts that getting our blood pumping helps all our organs get more oxygen and work more efficiently. These outside adventures will help you—physically, spiritually, and emotionally.

Keep moving!

Lesson Five: Live in the Present

*Dogs live in the spark of the moment
and take action now!*

Now is really all there is—this very moment. Yesterday's over. Tomorrow hasn't happened yet. So, here we are… this is it!

Dogs show us how to live in the present moment. They're not concerned with last week or last year, and they don't seem worried about tomorrow either. They're right here, right now. Whatever they decide to do… they're doing it in the present.

It's sometimes hard for us humans to live that way. Sure, we have many responsibilities and have to plan ahead, but it seems that we fall into the habit of living in the past or the future. We put off the exciting, challenging actions that will help us realize our dreams. Why do we put off those important actions? It's that four-letter word again… fear. It keeps us stuck.

It's easy to get bogged down with negative thinking—
focusing on what we don't have, rather than truly
appreciating what we do have. What we focus on
expands in our lives. If we fill our minds with news
stories of disaster and heartbreak around the globe, it
has a powerful effect on us. It's too much for anyone to
take in and process the world's pain when there's not
much that can be done about it.

Reminding ourselves over and over how much we do have to feel grateful about can do wonders for our attitude. Make it a habit.

Through their actions, our furry friends can teach us to greet every morning with a fresh view of hope and happiness. They appear to erase yesterday's inconveniences—a scary thunderstorm, a walk outside much later than expected, a rabies shot. Instead, there's the tail-wagging enthusiasm that THIS will be the best day ever!

Aren't they something?

Lesson Seven: Persistence

All success comes from persistence!

Dogs are persistent. They'll retrieve a ball countless times in a row. They'll go for walks as often as they can. They'll dig up a bone that's been buried for ages—all with a great spirit.

Many successful people didn't reach success on the merits of good grades, talent, or opportunity alone. It was by their unyielding persistence that they moved forward. My dad always used the term "stick-to-it-ive-ness" Is there such a word? Oh well, it works.

Our older dogs may develop some health issues and become arthritic, but their joy of life doesn't waver much. A ride in the car? You bet! Even if their legs aren't as strong at jumping into the back seat and they need a little boost, they persevere and finally make it. Success follows persistence!

Lesson Eight: Forgiveness

Dogs are the most forgiving creatures on earth.
What a lesson we can learn from them.

To forgive means to be in favor of giving, to grant free pardon. When we forgive another, we are also *giving* to ourselves. It's a mutual gift. It's also just as important to forgive ourselves—we are, after all, works in progress.

After we forgive, we need to go to the next step—to forget. We want to remember the lessons we learned, but we don't want to carry around heavy baggage from the past.

Our dogs demonstrate how to forgive and forget on a regular basis. If we accidentally step on a paw while they are napping on the floor, they might yelp and cry out in pain. Of course, we feel so sorry that it happened, but two minutes later, they're over it and moving on. When we leave the house without them, they look brokenhearted and pitifully sad. But when we return, it's back to happy tail wags… all is forgiven and forgotten.

*To err is human,
to forgive… is canine.*

— *Author Unknown*

Lesson Nine: Patience

*Dogs teach us to be content with
where we are right now.*

Since we were kids we've been told, "Be patient.
Wait. It'll be your turn soon." Sound familiar? And
how hard was it to be still and wait? We wanted to
open those presents *now*. We wanted to go out and
play *now*. We wanted that ice cream *now*. "Later"
wasn't an understandable option.

Through the years, I've often been told to take
action now and be persistent, while at the same time
knowing how important it is to relax, slow down,
and be patient. The real truth is that we need to do
both—be content right now and enjoy the journey
even as we patiently move forward.

If we don't enjoy the process, we probably won't
be happy when we arrive at our destination. Plus,
impatience is very stressful. It's fueled by thoughts
of *I should... what if...* and *if only.* Those frenzied
thoughts rob us of any pleasure we might derive
from the moment.

Experts agree that the more patient we are with ourselves and our circumstances, the more patient we are with others. That's a nice payoff and a great relief to those we've been impatient with.

One of the first things we learn in training our dogs is how important the "stay" command is. It's really all about patience.

We can all learn from this... to be patient and "stay." Stay in the moment, here and now.

Lesson Ten: Simplicity

*Dogs are a prime example of
truly living the simple life.*

If a crumpled up, empty envelope misses the trash can—*Yippee! A new toy.* Your dog will be all over it, having great fun dissecting it and shredding it beyond recognition. So much for fancy dog toys. Simple fun works.

Maybe we've gone so far into the philosophy of "more is better" that the pendulum is swinging back to the older days of simplicity. Many financially successful people who have or could afford just about anything have said that their greatest pleasures come from seeing their child's first school play or having a quiet morning to read or, yes, going on a long hike with their dog. Simple stuff.

We've gone over the top with adding complications to our lives with our "more" lifestyles. Somehow we've gotten the impression that not only will more material things enhance our lives, but the more we have, the more fulfilling our lives will be. In reality, the more we have, the more we have to insure, fix, store, clean, move around, and care for.

The very technology that seduced us with the promise of giving us more time by doing things faster actually keeps us constantly busy. With smart phones, tablets, and laptop computers, we can work from the beach, the cab, the park, and the plane. Whew… we need a break!

Dogs show us that it's hard, if not impossible, to be present in the glory of the moment without some degree of simplicity. They are content with the very basics: love, an uncomplicated bowl of food, water, countless naps, walks, and a playtime now and then. They give so much and expect so little.

Lesson Eleven: Friendship

What is a friend anyway? A buddy? A supporter?
Someone fun to hang out with?
A good listener? Someone who knows you well...
and still likes you? All of the above!

Dogs are dear, true friends, no matter what. They're right there to listen—they're our silent partners. They don't criticize what we say or do. They watch us grow, and we watch them grow. We have a bond.

Why are dogs considered man's best friend? They're loyal to the core. They don't judge us. They're endlessly entertaining. They're forgiving. They're protective. They love us unconditionally. Whew— that's a lot of reasons!

Our sweet angels teach us that the best way to have a true friend is to be one... any time of the day or night and in any season of life.

*No one appreciates the
very special genius
of your conversation
as the dog does.*

— *Christopher Morley*

Lesson Twelve: Aging

*In lots of ways,
dogs are mini-models of our lives.*

We can see in our dogs the aging process far easier than we can see it in ourselves. Since they age faster, we can learn a lot from them about our own aging.

I'll never forget the first time Cowgirl had to give up her attempts to jump up on the bed for a few soothing words and gentle pats before she curled up for the night. Her arthritis had progressed, but she had found new ways to adjust. My morning wake-up call had been her paw softly tapping my leg to remind me it was exactly 7:00 a.m. Now it turned into her tapping the side of the bed. It worked just fine.

Watching the aging process can help us be more accepting of it, even if we don't love the concept. It can be a sad and frustrating part of life. Aging reminds us of the loss of childhood and youth, loss of smooth, unwrinkled skin, and sometimes the loss of our health and our loved ones.

When the veterinarian casually mentioned in a routine checkup that along with arthritis, Cowgirl was losing some hearing and eyesight, I had a sinking feeling. He said it was typical of aging in dogs, no big deal.

No big deal? I beg your pardon, Doc. How could this strong, beautiful, vibrant creature be losing anything? It took time, but I finally began to accept the painful truth that we start aging the day we're born. I knew I had to feel the pain and move forward a day at a time.

We love our dogs through their aging process. That can help us love, accept, and be patient with others—and ourselves—through our own aging.

Lesson Thirteen: Love

Life is full of incredible adventures,
occasional disappointments,
and stunning successes.
There are ups and downs,
big victories, and a few tears.
But when all is said and done,
the most valuable lesson
I've learned in life is that
love is what matters most.

This chapter comes later in the book because after writing down all these lessons from Cowgirl, I now realize they've all been a lot about love.

Love is much more than a warm feeling. It's unconditional, positive regard. Giving and receiving love is a basic need… for all of us. It can be family love, romantic love, love of friends, or love of our dear pets.

Dogs love us no matter how absent-minded, uptight, busy, messy, cranky, late, or tired we might be. Their love for us never fades.

From their unconditional love, we can learn to have more unconditional love for ourselves. It's not always easy. Sometimes we have the erroneous notion that we must strive toward perfection to be more lovable. Our fur babies know we love them just the way they are.

We can only love others to the degree that we love ourselves. Think about it. Loving the self is not pride, arrogance, vanity, or self-centeredness. Love includes having great respect for ourselves—imperfections and all!

I'll never forget one bright, windy spring afternoon. Cowgirl and I were walking in a large field that was just beginning to turn green. The air smelled fresh and sweet. It had been a long winter, and even though her joint pain was increasing and her eyesight and hearing were going fast, Cowgirl ran around with as much gusto as she could muster. She savored every single minute.

As she ran toward me with her long blond hair and red bandana blowing in the wind, her loving eyes said, *Oh, thank you beyond measure!*

Love is not jealous or resentful. Love is feeling thankful that those you love are enjoying the moment. Our dogs can increase our capacity to love, and for that we can be eternally grateful.

Lesson Fourteen: Loss

*Sadly, our dogs give us the opportunity
to learn how to live through loss.*

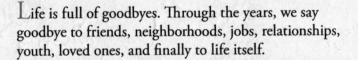

Life is full of goodbyes. Through the years, we say goodbye to friends, neighborhoods, jobs, relationships, youth, loved ones, and finally to life itself.

One day, you'll notice that your faithful, furry friend is just not the same. You'll have a veterinarian evaluate the symptoms, and you will hold on to hope. In fact, with treatment, there may be some improvement for a time. Everyone will be relieved!

But the truth is the end may be near… and it will happen either suddenly or slowly. It's a helpless feeling when our sweet pet's life is winding down. After all, they've been completely dependent on us, and now we have no solutions.

How do we say goodbye?

When Cowgirl was fading fast, the veterinary staff offered to carry her on a blanket to the small field behind the clinic so we could have time together outside—just the two of us.

The sky was the bluest I have ever seen. A few billowy, white clouds gave contrast, and a soft wind blew Cowgirl's flaxen hair.

As I lay on the grass beside her and we looked into each other's eyes, I thanked her for all she had given me over the years. She looked and listened intently as I reminded her of the joy, love, security, and wisdom she had showered me with. I tearfully told her that if she needed to move on to the next world, I would understand… or try to.

Just as I said that, Cowgirl wistfully looked away from me and up toward that beautiful sky. Her eyes followed the clouds… almost with an expression of longing.

Through my tears, I looked down at the grass between my fingers and into the face of a four-leaf clover. I picked it to save as a reminder of that bittersweet experience.

The next day, Cowgirl was given increased doses of morphine for her pain. Then I knew the time had come. I took a deep breath and told the doctor I was ready to let her go. I had to, for her. But I wanted it to be very special.

I placed a feather, a silver heart, and her red bandana on her shoulder as she lay quietly on her side. While the doctor slowly injected the final dose, I encouraged her spirit to have a smooth trip to heaven. After saying a prayer of thanks to God for creating her, I sadly kissed her goodbye. My heart had never been so heavy.

Losing our dear pets teaches us that death is as sure as life. They give us the opportunity to experience letting go of a part of our family… someone we dearly cherished and will hold close in our hearts forever.

Sometimes the most painful life experiences are the most profound.

A giving heart is open wide
to the needs of others.
It doesn't ask why, but when...
and it doesn't keep score.

A giving heart is never empty—
it's overflowing.
It responds through genuine caring
and gives with pure joy.

I am so grateful
you shared your giving heart
with me.

Lesson Fifteen: Healing

Learning how to grieve is a gift that can be helpful for the rest of our lives.

Our precious pets are woven into the fabric of our lives. They are an intimate part of us. They are part of our family. They are loving, fun, faithful, and true.

When they pass on, we may wonder how we will ever smile again. How will our hearts ever mend? It's a crushing blow.

There is hope through healing. Living with loss is a process, and it's not an easy one. Everyone walks his or her own healing pathway—in his or her own style. Loss can bring up many different emotions—sadness, anger, confusion, guilt, fear, and maybe even relief that our loved one is free of pain.

Mourning is important. It's a form of cleansing of the spirit. If we don't grieve, our extreme feelings get pushed aside, but they don't go away. They may pop up somewhere down the road and have an effect on us physically and emotionally.

Moving on doesn't mean that we're over it… all done. The cherished memories of our beloved pets will always be with us. Again, we must give ourselves all the time we need to get there.

Life does go on.

Exactly one week after Cowgirl's death, my phone rang. It was the veterinarian's office saying that several days before, someone had brought in a small dog who was lost and running down the highway. She reminded them of Cowgirl.

Since nobody claimed her, I accepted their invitation to just drop by and see her. Of course… that was it! We bonded immediately during that short visit. I named her Callie and I adopted her on the spot, knowing she needed a loving home. I needed her as much.

Callie didn't replace Cowgirl. She filled a new space in my life created out of the blue. Another angel! Callie is showing me the benefits of an open heart. Hmmm… I wonder what other lessons she will teach me.

Callie

About the Author

To say Carol has had a colorful background is a huge understatement! She lived in an eighteen-foot trailer as a child... surrounded by circus performers. After flunking out of three colleges, she was determined enough to pursue and ultimately earn a bachelor's degree in psychology and a master's degree in counselor education from New York University. She taught life skills and stress management before becoming a sought-after motivational speaker.

Carol is the author of the popular book *Get Fired Up Without Burning Out!* She also has an inspiring story in the million-selling *Chicken Soup for the College Soul*.

Carol has a stellar music background as well. She has performed with such entertainment legends as Johnny Cash, Roy Clark, Jimmy Buffett, and Willie Nelson. And as an actress, she has had movie roles with Faye Dunaway and Sandra Bullock.

In spite of all her accomplishments, Carol would say that she learned more practical life lessons from her dog Cowgirl than from any college course. *Pawprints of Wisdom* is a reminder of those powerful lessons about love, laughter, loss, patience, and more that we can learn from our furry friends.